Narcissism

Managing Manipulative Parents, Repairing Relationships, And Regaining Empathy Are All Topics That Are Covered In This Comprehensive Healing Guide

(Intellectual Discrimination And Colonial Narcissism)

Thomas Hellwig

TABLE OF CONTENT

Interactive Self-Reflection: 1

For their Personal Gain, they Utilise People. 14

METHODS TO ENSURE THAT THEY DO NOT CONTACT YOU 32

Disregarding or pardoning their bad behaviour 63

The Brain Underpinnings of Anxious Attachment . 80

What concrete or particular factors lead to narcissism? 100

The Influence of Words: Modifying the Internal Narrative 117

The Five Abuse Stages 140

Interactive Self-Reflection:

Accepting Personal Development and Taking on the Role of Change Architects

I beseech you to engage in a profoundly introspective moment. This private conversation reveals the deepest desires for self-improvement and metamorphosis hidden in the most private corners of your being. Are you prepared to boldly accept that something has to change and to fully commit to the journey toward empathy that will improve your life? Venture boldly into the unknown territories of your goals, anxieties, and wants. Accept the vulnerability and uncertainty that may surface because those are the hallowed places where profound change, personal development, and the cultivation of empathy—the very thing that unites us as human beings—happen.

Recall that the road to empathy requires an unflinching faith in our ability to change and an uncompromising commitment to personal development. We may unleash our infinite potential to rise above the limitations of narcissism and nurture the luminous flame of empathy when we accept the urgent need for change and welcome personal growth. We will go much further in the upcoming chapters, revealing powerful techniques, engaging activities, and illuminating perspectives that will lead you to a deep metamorphosis—a manifestation of empathy that comes from the core of your being.

Examining the Roots and Fundamental Causes of Narcissistic Attitudes

This insightful and very reflective section of our life-changing adventure will bravely delve into the roots and fundamental reasons for narcissistic tendencies. During this comprehensive session, we will delve into the complexities of self-understanding and carefully untangle the rich tapestry that gives rise to these tendencies. Get ready for a very human and contemplative journey as we explore the deepest recesses of the human psyche and uncover the many facets of who we are.

Revealing the Origins: Comprehending the Origins of Narcissism

Imagine a large, complex environment, a tapestry of our experiences, feelings, and upbringing. The roots of narcissistic tendencies are waiting to be found inside this kaleidoscope of interwoven threads. Let's go on an interactive adventure of self-discovery together, revealing more and more about ourselves as we immerse ourselves in the history of our lives.

a. Following the Threads: Discovering the Tapestry of Formative Encounters

Spend some time thinking back on the memories, encounters, connections, and influences that have molded you into who you are now. Can you pinpoint the turning points, the strands that entwine to form the intricate tapestry of your existence that might have aided in the emergence of narcissistic tendencies? By boldly following these threads, we can learn a great deal about the underlying causes of our actions and cognitive processes. Take part in this profoundly introspective investigation to uncover the buried remnants of your history and dissect the complex web that has molded how you see yourself and others.

b. Fostering Empathy: Accepting Your Inner Child's Empathy

It is important to develop compassion for yourself and the fragile inner child who may have endured trauma, abuse, or unfulfilled needs as we explore the roots of narcissistic tendencies. Can you provide comfort and forgiveness to the hurting aspects of yourself by showing them empathy and understanding? We may heal the wounds of the past, build the path for personal development, and foster empathy for others by tending to our inner child with compassion and love.

The acceptance of selfishness as a necessary characteristic in the corporate world highlights the challenges in defining and characterizing an individual with non-psychotic personality disorder (NPD); in many contexts, their behavior will resemble that of a highly successful person. This reasoning suggests that being selfish is a desirable—even necessary—quality for people who want to thrive.

Being completely selfish requires having no empathy or regard for other people's feelings; this is maybe the turning point from being viewed as socially "normal" to being diagnosed with a personality disorder. NPD sufferers are unable to develop empathy for others around them, which eventually makes it easier for them to control others because they are no longer able to respect their needs or feelings. Both psychopaths and people with NPD are linked to this kind of behavior.

It is important to realize that, like other personality traits, self-awareness and self-interest are crucial. Sometimes, it takes selfishness to ensure you follow your morals and principles or even just to finish a task dear to your heart. The key distinction is realizing the potential impact on others and deciding to proceed regardless of the psychological and physical repercussions. Being selfless means that you won't ever advocate for what you believe in, you'll probably spend your life going along with the crowd, and you might never reach your full potential.

It has been proposed that a harsh upbringing can contribute to adult selfishness. A child is prone to withdraw into their world if they receive little or no recognition or praise for their presence. Some of these kids may grow up to be social misfits and reclusive, while others will create imaginary worlds to escape life's harsh realities. Having the authority, respect, and control they lack as children is a common theme in many fantasy realms. These worlds can persist throughout adulthood, and when the need to be liked takes precedence over all other emotions, a narcissistic personality type will emerge. Once more, your genes and other factors will affect this development.

Although selfishness is a characteristic of people with NPD, selfishness is not a sign of NPD. Apart from the previously mentioned healthy kind of selfishness, most people become selfish due to the pressures and tensions in their own lives; this is a reaction to one's surroundings rather than a deep-seated desire to harm others. Although people with NPD are typically endearing and seem to fit in well, they are also highly accommodating. Selfish people tend to come across as selfish. This is a result of their ability to dominate and manipulate those around them to satisfy their egotistical desires. The distinguishing factor between an individual with NPD and a non-afflicted person is the obvious and crucial personality difference. Since appearing well to others is important to someone with true NPD, getting the assistance they require to reach their objectives will be ensured. Their charm and charisma will conceal their true nature and motivation from you, making them appear trustworthy and selfless when they are everything but.

7. Children

it is sometimes quite difficult for couples who have children together to leave. Additionally, concerns regarding guardianship can arise.

8. Fondness

Someone may be kept in a relationship by waiting for feelings of affection.

9. Money

If one partner depends on the other for financial support, this could complicate the exit plans.

Other plausible explanations are:

10. You No Longer Feel Confident

Walking out of a bad relationship can take a lot of confidence. Nonetheless, it could be difficult to stop by if a toxic partner has made fun of you or tired you out.

11. You Made A Huge Energy Contribution

It will be much harder to let go if it appears like you put a lot of effort into your relationship, which is often the case in negative situations.

"We've proactively been together for so long, I should stay," you may be thinking. Or, on the contrary, "I've put such a great amount into this relationship, I can't allow it to fall flat,"

In any case, that isn't a good enough reason to stay. In the unlikely event that this seems to be the primary reason you're hanging around, it will be beneficial to consider what you truly need, possibly with the help of a therapist.

12. It is impossible to imagine being apart from everyone else.

An unhealthy relationship can feel like your beginning and end because it can damage your confidence and the energy expected to make all the difference. This makes leaving it very difficult.

Even though ending an unhealthy relationship might be challenging, working on yourself and identifying the unfavorable beliefs holding you back can make the process much easier.

For their Personal Gain, they Utilise People.

Using people for one's benefit, or exploiting them is another sign of narcissistic personality disorder. Narcissists find that other people are simpler to take advantage of because they either adhere to their perception of being superior or because others firmly submit to their will because of how everyone else perceives and treats them highly. Someone with this illness finds it simple to take advantage of others since they believe they are superior to everyone else and possess superior intelligence. Because these people don't deserve respect, in their opinion, it makes sense to take advantage of them.

Once more, we have a symptom that easily relates to other ailments. Their persistent need for more stems from their assumption that they are entitled to what they are asking, which is the root of exploitation.

It's their habit to make fun of other people.

A narcissist frequently puts down other people in an attempt to appear superior and to cover up their feelings of inadequacy and inadequacies. They believe that, in contrast, this presents them to others as desirable and acceptable.

Narcissists may label their targets as "inferior" individuals, "clueless" managers, "flawed" friends or ex-spouses, or "inferior" people overall. They almost always speak about other people from a position of apparent superiority. Numerous individuals have experienced narcissistic employers.

Steer clear of Commitment.

When someone you are romantically interested in seems attractive and affectionate towards you but, after some time passes, decides not to pursue the connection further, it might be perplexing. The good news is that you may regain your dignity, equilibrium, and narcissistic personality disorder.

Self-Reliant

They'll overestimate how important they think they are and how much greater than others. This symptom can be easily recognized by boasting, inflating their value, and concentrating a lot on the things they believe are important. Because they perceive no reason not to, the person frequently denigrates others. Since they already perceive themselves as more significant and superior, they don't see any issue with bringing it up or assuming everyone knows it. To view oneself in this sense, nothing specific needs to happen or be there. Nothing can be done to change their mind because they already feel strongly about it. In social situations, they frequently try to take center stage or leave with the idea that they will be followed. They'll believe that people will follow their instructions or respect them immediately for their actions and words.

Section Three: Diagnoses

A qualified specialist is competent to identify narcissistic personality disorder. In addition to asking some additional in-depth inquiries, the professional will utilize the previously described symptoms as a general guide to evaluate your or a loved one's condition. A general practitioner or family physician is not usually qualified or prepared to identify a personality disorder. Hence, only a trained specialist should make the diagnosis. If they think you may have a personality issue, they will recommend you to the appropriate person to speak with.

Regretfully, no genetic, blood, or laboratory testing is available to diagnose this condition. Additionally, because they don't think they are sick, people with this illness typically avoid getting care. Individuals suffering from this disorder won't seek medical attention until the disorder starts to interfere with their personal or professional lives. This typically occurs when people are too stressed to handle life's events, and their coping mechanisms are depleted.

As a result, only mental health care providers can diagnose this illness, and they do so by comparing the patient's symptoms and life history. They will be the ones to determine if you qualify as a narcissist or not.

Examinations

The exam is relatively straightforward, and completing the tests is not too difficult. Since narcissism has no outward symptoms, a doctor will only take samples or draw blood if they suspect you have a medical condition. If not, a psychological assessment, signs, and symptoms will be used to diagnose.

It's not uncommon to have more than one personality disorder identified at once, and the characteristics of narcissism can often be confused with other signs of distinct personality disorders.

Getting Ready for the Consultation

If you do not know of a psychologist to consult, you should first make an appointment with your primary care physician. They will help you find the right person to consult to receive a diagnosis or examine your mental health.

How to Proceed

Prior to the session, you ought to jot down the following items:

Symptoms that you may have experienced or are experiencing, together with the duration of their prevalence. List the causes of these symptoms that you are aware of together with your symptoms. What, for instance, causes you to feel angry or discouraged?

Personal details like terrible experiences in the past or a significant stressor in your life that could be aggravating your disease.

Medical data that contains a history of your physical and mental health as well as problems for which you have received a diagnosis.

You may be taking Vitamins, minerals, medications, and the dose levels you're ingesting. Unbelievably, prescription or over-the-counter drugs can have major negative consequences on mental health, including what may appear to be narcissism.

You could pose A set of inquiries to your mental health professional to initiate the recovery process.

You should bring a trusted family member to your appointment to feel more secure. Additionally, you should have them present so they can recall the specifics. Additionally, you might want to confirm that the person will be able to ask insightful questions and provide the psychologist with knowledge that could be crucial because they have likely known you for a long time.

Examining the Causes and Initiations of Narcissistic Conduct

Gaining knowledge about the causes of narcissistic behavior helps explain why people exhibit these behaviors. Prominent psychoanalysts Heinz Kohut and Otto Kernberg's clinical theories provide insight into the intricate interactions between early events and relationships that lead to the development of narcissistic personality traits in maturity.

Heinz Kohut's Point of View

Kohut highlights how early relationships—especially those with parents—have a significant impact on how narcissistic behavior develops. Kohut argues that a kid's self-concept develops due to interactions with other people, especially with their primary carer, frequently their mother. These interactions give the child the vital opportunity to feel validated, approved of, and able to identify with good role models. By "mirroring," empathetic and caring parents help their children see their strengths and weaknesses, forming a more realistic self-image. Moreover, Kohut claims that when children see their parents' flaws and limits, they internalize a positive, healthy self-image. However, a child's self-development is hampered when parents lack empathy or neglect to provide the required validation and role modeling, which leads to a static and false self-concept. According to Kohut, a fundamental aspect of narcissistic behavior is this developmental pause, when people uphold grandiose self-views and continue to idealize others in order to boost their self-esteem.

Otto Kernberg's Point of View

On the other hand, narcissism, according to Kernberg's hypothesis, is a defense mechanism that results from parental neglect and is marked by a lack of empathy and coldness. The youngster experiences emotional hunger due to this neglect, which fuels resentment and dissatisfaction. According to Kernberg, children who experience this emotional emptiness may develop narcissistic defense mechanisms. As a result, taking solace in the parts of themselves that attract praise and interest from others. Ultimately, this defensive strategy leads to an exaggerated and grandiose self-concept as people try to compensate for the emptiness they felt in their first relationships. Kernberg's perspective emphasizes the notion that narcissists struggle with self-worth issues on the inside while projecting an air of confidence and grandiosity on the outside.

Essentially, Kohut and Kernberg agree that early interactions and experiences have a significant influence on the emergence of narcissistic behavior. These theories offer complex frameworks for understanding the complex roots of narcissism, whether through disturbances in self-development or defensive reactions to neglect. Understanding these elements adds to a more detailed understanding of how and why people display narcissistic behavior, helping to uncover the nuances underlying it.

WHAT MAKES NARCISSISTS TICK, CHAPTER THREE

Mature consciences are typically absent from narcissists. Their biggest concern is getting penalized or having their reputations tarnished in any way. Indeed, they are frequently devout and gloomy as hell.

Like the mythical Narcissus, narcissists frequently place a great deal of importance on appearances—both their own and others—and in order to maintain their façade, they frequently lie. A narcissist would sooner claim to be employed by the White House than acknowledge that he hasn't had a job in a long time.

They are horrible listeners and enjoy talking about themselves, so when you start talking, they frequently tune you out or glaze over—unless you are talking about them. They cannot see why stopping everything you do to give them your undivided attention would be more important than everything else. They take great pleasure in receiving constant praise.

It's not always easy to identify a narcissist at first glance because they tend to blend in with their surroundings. It is hardly likely that the egotistical local farmer will be as visible as the egotistical senior attorney. Furthermore, some narcissists conceal this aspect of themselves and pretend to be kind until Mr. Jekyll reveals his hairy face because they identify as extremely devout and pious.

Narcissists can project drastically different personas at home, work, church, and retail establishments.

Narcissists rarely examine themselves; instead, they are more fascinated by the outside world. This innate resistance to any kind of self-examination may be what has made it so difficult for them to overcome their problem.

Narcissists are typically too enthusiastic, aggressive, and, yes, competitive. They also tend to have an overabundance of energy. Narcissistic personalities have a strong propensity to be bullies; if you don't have a backbone and defend yourself, they will treat you as badly as possible. They often don't pause to consider it, so it's not even intentional. It happens naturally, and you end up with the worst of it.

The majority of narcissists are products of nurture rather than nurturing itself. I assure you that this is not the time to blame the parents for their narcissism. The causes of narcissism are circumstances, experiences, and—above all—choice. Individualsdecidedecide to acquire particular habits, which quickly become a part of who they are.

It's just one of the strange wirings in their nature for narcissists to be so sensitive to criticism, both of themselves and other people.

METHODS TO ENSURE THAT THEY DO NOT CONTACT YOU

Embrace them from a distance.
No, just because a friend or spouse turns out to be a narcissist does not mean that I have encouraged you to leave your friendship with them, file for divorce, or quit your job. The finest of us experience it, and as with most things in life, narcissists are plentiful, so the grass isn't necessarily greener on the other side. When you love someone from a distance, it doesn't mean you have to ignore them when they want to come over for dinner; it just means you must adjust your

viewpoint and attitude. I promise you that you won't get emotional support from them; therefore, you need to be careful not to rely on them for anything. It implies that you must accept that you are powerless to alter who they are and that trying to do so will only cause you harm. In addition, they frequently deny that they require assistance. They simply believe they are better than everyone else, and you are either too naive or jealous to recognize them for their worth.

Pardon and continue to pardon until it can no longer control you.

Despite their best efforts to persuade you otherwise, narcissism, in all honesty, speaks more about the individual exhibiting it than it does about you, the helpless onlooker, who has to witness it. Acquire the skill of forgiveness and maintain it until it no longer influences you. Recognize that narcissists endure excruciating agony. Even when someone is unsure of the precise term to describe their behavior or condition, most people find it extremely off-putting. Narcissists frequently wind up isolating themselves from friends, families, and coworkers until they are by themselves. Though they may not seem to notice, trust me when I say they do; they simply don't know how to adjust very often.

Make a space map for yourself.

The awful thing about narcissists is that they make it incredibly simple to be destroyed by them. Without learning to set boundaries and demand your own time and space, the narcissist will subdue you with the delicacy of a steamroller. Narcissists are adept at manipulating situations so that you feel responsible for their abuse or neglect of you. When they leave you emotionally bloody on the ground, you will only be responsible for yourself if you let them get inside.

Recognize that you are not a failure.

A narcissist can easily destroy a good, powerful, self-assured, well-groomed person; chances are that if you ended up in a tangle with one, you were never a loser in the first place.

Come on, were you alone in a cave with only ants for company before that person entered your life? Just that! You were a person with a life, a purpose, desires, and objectives that you were probably close to accomplishing. Nobody can characterize you unless

Keep an eye on yourself.

Yes, I do mean that in the literal sense. Narcissists are experts at manipulating; it's in their nature; they can't help it. You must keep a close eye on yourself to ensure you aren't falling for one of their extravagant ideas. If you must, make sure that many other people surround you to mitigate the negative effects of spending needless time with them.

Additionally, you should start intentionally keeping an eye on your self-perception because, if there's one thing you can be sure of, it's that if your mental patterns are based on poor self-worth, you will come into contact with a lot of narcissists. Make sure you're not telling yourself inadvertently that narcissists are the only people you deserve.

You rarely can compete with a narcissist if you are not one yourself. Thus, you should not have to live among narcissists in your life.

1.2 The Deep Meaning of Matrimony

God's plan for marriage goes far beyond satisfying one's wishes or following social conventions. It serves as a significant means by which people set out on a life-changing adventure that has an incredibly inspiring impact on their own lives and those around them.

➢ Support and emotional companionship

Fundamentally, matrimony is a heavenly connection that forges an enduring friendship between two spirits. It offers a haven of love and understanding when two people set out on a common path, fostering affection, emotional support, and a strong sense of identity. People navigate the ups and downs of life together in this partnership, finding comfort in each other's company.

➢Creating a family and having children

Matrimony serves as a vehicle for procreation in the divine plan of creation, which also ensures the survival of the human race. When two people get married, they form a family that raises the next generation by giving them a secure and caring environment in which to grow up. In this sense, marriage is crucial to determining how humanity will develop in the future.

➢ Spiritual Development and Equivalent Metamorphosis

Marriage is an amazing furnace for spiritual development. When two individuals get together, they embark on self-exploration and develop their forbearance, empathy, and fortitude. They rely on one another's everlasting love and support as they work together to become the finest versions of themselves. Marital struggles and victories provide stepping stones for growth on the inside and outside, creating a deep bond that transcends this world.

➤ Stability of Society

Matrimony is not only a private commitment; it is essential to the stability of society. A healthy and flourishing community is built on strong marriages. They give kids a stable environment to grow up and help them develop common ideals, devotion, and a feeling of duty. People are more likely to find security, support, and the foundation to follow their aspirations in a society that values marriage.

➤ The Image of God Reflected

The divine plan is reflected in marriage. When two people come together, they reflect the deep unity of God's love and exemplify the harmonious duality that permeates the cosmos. The holy image is made visible via the union of two unique souls, and the power of love is visible to everyone.

Making Time for Your Passions

You have probably never been allowed to spend time doing the things you enjoy for as long as you have been in a relationship with the narcissist. If you did, your narcissistic partner most certainly heavily conditioned and controlled it. You might, therefore, experience a wide range of feelings, including confusion, guilt, and shame, when engaging in your favorite activities. But you have to get started. You can feel more deserving of yourself if you give yourself enough time to gradually return to the things you love to do. However, it can also help you feel more confident when you do these things.

When you first resume doing what you love, you can experience many feelings. These sensations could include intense thoughts of inadequacy that make you feel as though you no longer desire to participate in these activities. You need to deal with the source of these feelings.

There's a significant likelihood that your CPTSD and trauma bond are the reasons behind your desire to stop engaging in these activities. Commit to engaging in the activities you used to enjoy for a predetermined period, and make sure you stick with it for the whole timeframe you determined upfront to determine whether this is truly your distaste or the product of your conditioning. After that time has passed, review your pledge. Try to find a different hobby to substitute if you still don't enjoy doing that one.

It's not necessary to pursue all of your passions at once. Start with two things and take your time. One can be larger, such as a passion project or pastime, and smaller, such as enjoying your favoritetea or reintroducing a tiny piece of your daily routine that makes you happy. Starting with these two simple commitments will allow you to gradually return to your favorite activities without feeling overburdened. You can then add on more as you start feeling more at ease and competent with these hobbies until you are doing everything you enjoy again. You are in charge and free to slow down and make adjustments if you ever start feeling overburdened by everything on your plate. Ensure you attend to your needs, maintain clarity, and focus on their needs. Your needs were seldom satisfied or taken care of when you were in an abusive relationship. Ignoring them might, therefore, cause worry and anxiety. On the other hand, paying them more attention than usual can have the same effect. It's crucial to take it slow and give yourself the room and time to reassess.

Concentrating on Your Diet and Exercise

Our desire for exercise and nutrition are the first things we usually forget about when we are experiencing stress in our lives. Neglecting these might be an indication of extreme stress. However, it can also happen when we cease taking care of ourselves in favor of someone else, like in an abusive relationship. When you are coming out of a serious relationship that involves abuse, it is important to focus on your nutrition and fitness regimen. Greatly assist your body and mind by providing them with the necessary nutrients to overcome everyday stress and its associated symptoms.

It is a good idea to think about joining an exercise class or a group with other people who will work out with you for your fitness needs. This can help you maintain your commitment and help you retrain your social skills to function outside of your abusive relationship. Making new acquaintances, connections, and friends can be energizing. These people are unlikely to be aware of any negative information your ex-partner may be disseminating about you through smear campaigns because they do not know your ex-partner. Furthermore, you may be yourself around them because they do not consider you to be a "abused person." This independence, combined with a fresh, health-conscious workout routine, can be immensely beneficial for anyone returning from an abusive relationship.

Additionally, you need to confirm that you are eating healthfully. Because of the stress, people in abusive relationships either overeat or undereat. You will need to select a healthy diet plan to assist you in eating a nutritious, well-balanced diet suitable for your needs, depending on which of the above you struggle with.

When you are recovering from the emotional and psychological aftereffects of abuse, there are additional nutrients that you may take advantage of to support your mood. Omega fatty acids, niacin, and vitamins B and D are all recognized to support improved mental health and mood enhancement. Including these in your diet can help you feel better overall, allowing you to start enjoying your healing journey and living a more joyful life daily.

This entails being able to recognize, understand.

People can respond to subversive ways of behaving with grace and compassion by honing their ability to comprehend people at their core. This advances a meaningful exchange rather than inciting conflict.

Furthermore, defining boundaries is essential to preventing and treating serious sabotage.

Defining personal boundaries and presumptions facilitates the development of a respectful working environment. Firm boundaries reduce the possibility of destructive behaviors flourishing and create an environment where individuals feel truly protected and respected.

A favorable mental image of oneself is essential to succeeding in close-to-home subversion.

Believing in oneself and appreciating it independently of other people's approval can be a powerful defense against project failure.

This assurance fortifies individuals against negative effects and facilitates the development of stronger relationships.

Close-to-home undermining is generally a delicate dance within the realm of interpersonal relationships.

It entails recognizing, addressing, and overcoming behaviors obstructing prosperity in one's immediate surroundings. By accepting compassion, empathy, strong boundaries, and mindfulness, individuals can investigate this complex dance and create bonds that support individual growth and group support.

1. Introspection: The first step to mastering profound sabotaging is

introspection. Individuals should examine their motives, shortcomings, and patterns of behavior to raise awareness of the potential effects of their actions on other people. This consideration paves the way for self-awareness and a more confident approach to handling relationships.

2. Sympathy as a Counterforce: Reacting compassionately to personal sabotage can disrupt harmful patterns. Comprehending that disruptive behaviors often stem from personal struggles enables individuals to approach conflicts with empathy. This shift in context opens the door to fruitful communication and mutual comprehension.

3. Powerful Correspondence: The art of undermining close to home is undermined by transparent correspondence. Encouraging a culture of direct communication within relationships addresses fundamental problems and reduces the likelihood of distant, aggressive behaviors. The goal of this discussion should be to consider one another's points of view and reach a worthwhile consensus.

4. Constructing Nearby Flexibility: Mastering extreme adaptability is essential to long-term subversive projects. This entails appreciating strengths, accepting criticism, and learning from setbacks. Promoting a flexible mindset makes people less

vulnerable to the negative impact of destroying behavioral patterns.

5. Defining and Enforcing Limits: Well-defined boundaries serve as a powerful deterrent against subversion that occurs close to home. Individual borders are drawn and communicated to create a setting where people feel valued and respected. This proactive approach improves the partnership dynamic by reducing the possibility of undermining behaviors taking hold.

6. Developing a Positive Mental Self-Portrait: Reaffirming self-confidence without regard to external validation is important. Building a good mental image of oneself provides a solid foundation against attempts to undermine certainty.

Acknowledging progress, practicing self-empathy, and celebrating successes contribute to a flexible identity.

7. Unending Personal Development: The journey to become a master at local subversion is an ongoing process of self-discovery. Adopting an attitude of continuous improvement enables individuals to adapt, learn from experiences, and improve their interpersonal skills. This commitment to self-improvement fosters deeper, more fulfilling relationships.

The field of profound subversion encompasses a broad range of techniques, including introspection, empathy, persuasive communication, adaptability, boundary-setting, constructive self-perception, and ongoing self-development.

By incorporating these elements into routine conversations, individuals can investigate the nuances of relationships with a greater sense of awareness, adaptability, and respect.

Team-building exercises enhance the resilience and cohesion of a team. Leaders must acknowledge the importance of team-building activities in cultivating favorable relationships, enhancing communication, and establishing trust within the team. Beyond simple games and activities, team building entails deliberate attempts to establish a welcoming and encouraging team environment. Leaders must evaluate the efficacy of current team-building tactics and modify them to suit their groups' distinct requirements and dynamics.

Social ties among teammates support a feeling of unity and acceptance. Leaders must foster formal and casual social contact among team members, enabling them to establish personal connections. Building social ties mitigates the individuality and loneliness that are frequently linked to narcissistic tendencies. Leaders need to consider how they contribute to fostering a culture on the team where members are at ease discussing personal matters and forming bonds that go beyond work-related activities.

Resilient team dynamics achieve the delicate balance between autonomy and collaboration. Leaders must consider how much freedom they provide their team members while ensuring that working together is still a top priority. Maintaining a healthy balance between autonomy and teamwork inhibits the growth of narcissistic tendencies linked to excessive individuality or micromanagement. Leaders must encourage a culture that promotes teamwork while enabling team members to take responsibility for their job.

Team accomplishments must be aggressively acknowledged and celebrated by leaders. When considering how often the team recognizes its accomplishments, evaluating how inclusive and frequent these activities are is important. Acknowledging collective accomplishments strengthens a supportive team environment and reduces the likelihood of people turning to narcissistic actions to seek approval. Leaders are responsible for ensuring that recognition reflects the company's principles and highlights the team's collaborative accomplishments.

To stop narcissistic behaviors from developing, leaders need to evaluate the power relationships in their teams. Understanding the distribution of authority, influence, and decision-making is necessary in reflecting on power dynamics. By intentionally minimizing hierarchical systems that could exacerbate power disparities, leaders can create a climate where team members feel encouraged to contribute without worrying about being taken advantage of or retaliated against.

Resilient dynamics in teams depend on accountability. Leaders must consider the team's commitment to accountability to guarantee that every team member accepts responsibility for their contributions and deeds. Fostering an environment where accountability is valued reduces the probability that people may turn to narcissistic actions to escape accountability or assign blame. For the team to succeed, leaders must set an example of accountability and promote shared responsibility.

A case study on developing resilient team dynamics can be found in Google's approach to team effectiveness. A culture of resistance to narcissistic behaviors exists in the workplace when psychological safety, open communication, and recognition of various contributions are prioritized. This case study emphasizes the importance of deliberately fostering an atmosphere where teams can flourish via cooperation, trust, and common objectives.

The innovative team dynamics at Pixar provide a case study for collaborative creation. Open communication, a diversity of viewpoints, and a common dedication to artistic excellence are all encouraged by Pixar's culture. This case study highlights how strong team dynamics support an organizational culture that challenges compartmentalized thinking frequently connected to selfish actions. Leaders can learn from Pixar's accomplishments in fostering a team atmosphere where the individual contributions of every team member are recognized.

Team facilitators are roles that leaders need to embrace. Evaluating how leaders foster diversity, communication, and collaboration within their teams is crucial to reflect on this job. It takes deliberate leadership to foster an atmosphere where team members feel appreciated, empowered, and committed to achieving common objectives. Understanding the significance of their facilitation role guarantees that leaders actively support resilient team dynamics that thwart the rise of narcissistic tendencies.

Disregarding or pardoning their bad behaviour

Narcissists never take ownership of their actions and often invent excuses for why hurting or discrediting someone is acceptable. Continually, their victim will take the blame for them or offer an apology for their initial inappropriate behavior. In response, a victim can say something like, "They are just stressed out right now," or "You are not as familiar with them as I am."

High-class and haughty stations

A selfish person's inflated tone and significance allow little opportunity for others to vary, which isolates the other party from the connection. Narcissists are ill-suited to form relationships because they cannot connect with others, which makes the other person in the relationship feel ignored or unheard. In the end, you'll learn to keep your emotions to yourself or to talk about the things in your life.

Acts of Aggression

Narcissists are masters at manipulating other people's feelings. Manipulative narcissists will influence your thoughts and desires. The most common form of manipulation is gaslighting, while additional options include emotional blackmail and promises of the future. Manipulation can lead to confusion, low self-esteem, anxiety, embarrassment, and guilt. You can also be convinced to stay in bed, neglect your job, have sex, or give the narcissist money.

Using the victim role

When all else fails, the narcissist plays the victim card. This is done to win people over and further control behavior. Despite having a strong and dominant personality, narcissists will often play the victim when they are criticized to gain sympathy and appear weaker. Furthermore, the narcissist can avoid taking responsibility for their acts by placing the blame on their environment.

Exploitation: For a narcissist, the goal of other people is to fulfill their desires. They will take advantage of people without feeling guilty or embarrassed.

They don't think about how their actions can affect others, making their victims feel rejected and abandoned.

sweeping

This is the process of "sucking" someone back into a relationship, usually following a period of silent treatment. Hoovering has also been compared to emotional blackmail. If the narcissist feels that they are losing control, they will change their approach. They will support you, get close to you, or lift your spirits. As soon as things go better and the victim thinks the narcissist has changed, they immediately go back to their abusive ways.

Calm Handling

Silent treatments are a cruel kind of emotional abuse that is applied to victims as punishment. While not everyone who receives the silent treatment suffers from NPD, it is never a good idea to settle conflicts in this way.

Seeking Assistance: Counselling, Support Communities, and Setting Limits

There are several advantages to therapy. Gaining perspective on one's experiences is one of the benefits of therapy for the individual. People become more aware of their current relationship with their narcissistic parent and start to comprehend the dominant/submissive dynamics between them and their parent. We can better handle our narcissistic parents with the help of therapy. Counselors assist clients by teaching them how to establish new boundaries for themselves. They also give you a secure space to communicate your feelings and have your experiences validated. There's much more to therapy than simply listening.

People gain from support groups in the same way that drug abusers profit from 12-step meetings. Individuals in narcissistic support groups gather in person, over the phone, or via online chat rooms. Support groups provide people with a feeling of belonging and community. They offer hope, strength, and experience in coping with others who have similar problems. It is indescribable how healing it may be to relate to those who have experienced similar situations. People from all diverse backgrounds attend narcissistic support groups, but they are all united by the fact that they are coping with a selfish individual or people in their lives. Ideas and opinions are exchanged. The liberation a client experiences when they can finally state, "My father's exactly like that," can be a powerful first step towards healing from an adult narcissistic parent. It feels so good to be able to share at last. Being a part of a community can be a powerful healing force. We can now reach out and ask for and provide assistance because we no longer feel we are the only ones dealing with these problems.

One of the things that most survivors learn in therapy or support groups is how to set boundaries. Regaining control over your life is possible when you establish personal limits. What lies outside of our lives is defined by boundaries. There are several methods to draw boundaries. Here are a few examples of how they are configured: decreased interaction. It does not always imply no interaction. It does, however, entail avoiding as much interaction with this individual as possible. Why subject yourself to agony? Please give them a call once a week. Setting boundaries for communication and refusing to give in to the drama and manipulation of others are important boundaries.

Seek assistance and move elsewhere.

If you're going to be in a relationship with a narcissist, be honest with yourself about what you might reasonably expect. A narcissist won't transform into someone who truly values you, making you want to search elsewhere for emotional support and personal growth.

Examine the characteristics of and experiences in healthy relationships. If your family is narcissistic, you might not have a good understanding of what constitutes a positive, give-and-take relationship. You may also find the narcissistic dysfunctional sample to be comfortable. Remember that even while it feels familiar, it makes you feel awful. In a mutually beneficial relationship, you could feel valued, heard, and liberated to be who you are.

Spend time with people that let you see yourself as you truly are. Spending time with people who accept you for who you truly are and who understand your thoughts and emotions can help you maintain perspective and prevent you from falling for the narcissist's distortions.

If necessary, form new friendships outside of the narcissist's social circle. If you wish to control others more highly, some narcissists isolate the people in their lives. If this is your situation, you should dedicate time to mending broken friendships or developing new ones.

Seek meaning and purpose in your activities, volunteer work, and employment. Seek meaningful activities that make use of your skills and allow you to contribute, rather than depending on the narcissist to confirm your sense of self.

How to get away from a narcissist

It can be particularly difficult to end a relationship with a narcissist since, at least initially, they can be quite charming and charismatic, especially if you threaten to leave. It's acceptable to appear confused by the deceptive actions of the narcissist, to be engrossed in their desire for acceptance, or even to feel "gaslighted" and unsure of your discernment. If you are codependent, your decision to be trustworthy might take precedence over your desire to maintain your sense of security and identity. But it's important to remember that no one should have to endure verbal and emotional abuse, threats, or bullying when dating. There are ways to begin the repair process and let go of the narcissist, as well as the guilt and self-blame.

Learn about the symptoms of narcissistic personality disorder. The more knowledge you have, the more adept you will be at deciphering the tactics a narcissist might employ to keep you in the dating relationship. A narcissist will frequently revive the flattery and adulation (also known as "love bombing") that piqued your interest in them in the first place, even when you threaten to leave. Alternatively, they may offer lofty assurances about altering their behavior, which they have no intention of keeping. Put your reasons for quitting in writing. You can avoid getting lured back into the relationship by being explicit about your reasons for wanting to end it. Store your list somewhere accessible, such as on your phone, and consult it when self-doubt creeps in, or the narcissist is trying to seduce you with unrealistic promises.

During the time you spent together, the narcissist might have also damaged your bonds with friends and family or limited your social interactions. But regardless of your situation, I'm not alone anymore. If you are unable to contact your old friends, you may be able to get support from support organizations, domestic abuse hotlines, and shelters.

Avoid making baseless threats. Accepting the narcissist's transaction and, when you're ready, essentially walking away is a better strategy. Making declarations or threats will only serve to alert the narcissist and hinder your ability to escape.

Features of Nervous Attachment

In human relationships, certain patterns and behaviors stand out and serve as markers to provide light on the complex dance of desires and emotions. The universe of the anxiously attached person is like a symphony. Still, unlike the symphonies of most other people, theirs has intricate rhythms of anxiety and longing mixed in with notes of heightened emotions. To fully comprehend this, we must investigate the particular traits that characterize anxious attachment.

Think of a relationship as a boat navigating a huge emotional ocean. Most of the time, there is little to no turbulence, and the seas remain tranquil. However, for those who are nervously attached, the seas are frequently turbulent, with waves of uncertainty smashing against the ship or their perception of the connection, with every apparent chilly move or pause in time. A missed call triggers a cascade of thoughts that cast doubt on the strength of the link; it's not just a missed call. An unread message may indicate declining interest rather than being a simple mistake.

The heart that is eagerly attached is a delicate one. It is loved with an unmatched intensity and feels profound. However, this devotion is entwined with a persistent need for validation. The world appears to them frequently in extremes—either as a desert of neglect or an oasis of love. This viewpoint reflects their internal emotional landscape, sculpted by early relationships and past experiences rather than a deliberate decision.

In addition to the ongoing need for validation, heightened sensitivity to the emotional moods of others, particularly intimate partners, is another characteristic of anxious attachment. They can frequently detect mood swings and pick up on nuances others might miss. Deeply sympathetic connections can be facilitated by this emotional knowledge but can also cause anguish if overanalyzed or misread.

When we consider these traits, it becomes clear that comprehending anxious attachment involves more than just identifying patterns—it also entails understanding the underlying emotions. Every worried thought has an underlying need for validation and connection. A heartache for constancy and security accompanies every hesitation.

The Brain Underpinnings of Anxious Attachment

The human brain is an amazing natural system with a complex network of synapses and neurons. It controls our feelings, memories, ideas, and actions. But it's more than just a biological organ;

it's the medium through which our experiences in life are painted, forming our viewpoints and determining how we connect with others. In examining the field of anxious attachment, it is critical to comprehend how the brain mediates this specific form of relationship.

The early years of childhood are a time of fast brain development. This period results in the formation of neural connections that set the stage for later emotional, cognitive, and behavioral patterns. Envision a forest with multiple pathways. The less-traveled roads grow overgrown, while the ones you take more often become more distinct and easy to follow. Similarly, recurrent experiences—particularly those emotionally charged—strengthen particular neural pathways in the brain and increase their dominance.

Early experiences with uneven caregiving can cause the brain to become wired for alertness in persons with anxious attachment. Stress hormones are released more often in reaction to perceived dangers or uncertainties. In maturity, this hypervigilance might show itself as a persistent need for validation, a dread of abandonment, and an exaggerated reading of little interpersonal setbacks.

Furthermore, a few key hormones and neurotransmitters influence attachment behaviors. Of these, oxytocin is the most important. It is released during intimate physical contact, encouraging attachment and bonding. Any deviation from the regular patterns of oxytocin release, such as extended absences or decreased intimacy, can exacerbate feelings of anxiety and misery in those who are extremely attached.

But biology isn't the only factor. Since our brains are flexible, our past experiences don't have to define who we are or what happens to us. Because of this plasticity, we can rewire ingrained habits and create new ones that foster connection, trust, and security if we have the necessary awareness, comprehension, and work.

The neuroscience of attachment emphasizes a message of hope while also explaining the "why" underlying certain actions. We understand that our brains are flexible and that the correct treatments make healing and transformation possible.

How the Mind Handles Feelings

Emotions constitute an essential aspect of the human experience, encompassing intricate psychological and physiological responses to specific stimuli. They affect our choices, alter our views, and mold our relationships. However, how precisely does the brain process these feelings? Let's take a trip around the brain networks that underlie emotion.

1. Initial Response and Sensory Input: Every emotional reaction starts with an experience. Our sensory organs pick up

on stimuli first, whether a heartfelt movie scene, a well-known perfume, or a loved one's voice. The brain's sensory relay station, the thalamus, receives this information afterward. The data travels in two directions from the thalamus. A faster pathway passes through the sensory cortex and ends up directly in the amygdala. This dual-pathway mechanism allows us to process emotions quickly—such as leaping at the sound of a loud noise—while also taking our time to process emotions more deeply.

2. The Amygdala's Function: As was already established, the processing of emotions is largely dependent on the amygdala. It assesses the stimulus's

emotional value after receiving sensory input. Does it pose a threat? Is it an award? This assessment indicates that the amygdala elicits a suitable emotional reaction. For example, it may trigger a fear reaction in response to a perceived threat, readying the body for possible harm.

3. Prefrontal Cortex-Mediated Emotional Regulation: Although the prefrontal cortex (PFC) adds a layer of cognitive judgment to the process, the amygdala reacts quickly and instinctively. The PFC evaluates the amygdala's reaction by considering the situation, prior knowledge, and logical reasoning. Subsequently, it can adjust the emotional response, increasing or

decreasing it. For instance, the amygdala may immediately produce a terror response when it perceives a coiled object in the forest and interprets it as a snake. Based on contextual cues, the PFC may identify it as a coiled rope and ease the original dread.

4. Memory and the Hippocampus: Memories and emotions are closely entwined. Emotions are linked to particular memories via the hippocampus, which is also responsible for creating and recalling memories. Because of this, some stimuli can elicit strong emotional responses depending on prior experiences. A certain music could remind you of a happy day in the

past, or the smell of a dish might bring back memories of your early years.

NARCISSISTIC PERSONALITY DISORDER CAUSES

several different causes rather than a single one. Among these are:

1. Early Life Experiences: According to research, NPD may develop as a result of events that occurred during childhood. These experiences can include not having emotional support or validation as a child, having a loved one reject or criticize you, being abused or neglected, getting too much praise, growing up without limits and discipline, or having overly protective parents. Furthermore, traumatic experiences may also be relevant.

2. Genetics: Since NPD often runs in families, there may be a genetic component to the condition. Certain genes have been linked in studies to a higher risk of NPD and other psychiatric disorders. The risk of getting NPD may increase if certain genes are inherited from one or both parents. It's crucial to understand that while a family history of the illness may raise the risk of developing symptoms, it does not ensure that narcissism will manifest.

3. Cultural and Environmental Factors: A person's upbringing might impact the emergence of specific personality traits, such as those linked to NPD. The emphasis on individualism, power, achievement, and self-importance in

individualistic cultures may be a factor in the increased frequency of narcissistic tendencies. In contrast, collectivist cultures—that place a higher value on the needs of the collective than on the needs of the individual—tend to be less selfish.

4. Biological causes: NPD may be influenced by several biological causes. Increased oxidative stress, or an unbalanced concentration of damaging free radicals and antioxidants in the body, is a common symptom of NPD. Furthermore, brain scans may indicate anatomical changes in NPD patients, such as decreased gray matter in brain regions linked to empathy, emotional control, and compassion.

NARCISSISTIC GIRLS VS. GIRLS

Symptoms of a Narcissistic Female Individual

martyrdom Narcissistic women are frequently portrayed as victims or martyrs. They think that their pain is greater than that of everyone else. This is commonly known as latent or insecure narcissism, which is the manifestation of narcissistic qualities less ostentatiously.

Aesthetic: Female narcissists exhibit extreme vapidity, as do most narcissists. Somatic narcissism is the term for those who, to hide their flaws or fears, are fixated on their appearance and social presence.

Rivalrous and jealous - Narcissist women are known for their fierce competition. They want to be the most successful, attractive, smartest, and endearing women in the room. The female narcissist may harass other women to keep them out of the social group if they think they are more attractive or dangerous. They can do this to their partners, children, and even coworkers.

Domineering caregivers: When trying to discipline her children, a narcissistic mother may be unduly manipulative and in control. They consider themselves to be situational specialists.

The connection between physical symptoms and NPD

NPD has negative effects on physical health in addition to its other negative aspects. This particularly applies to men. Even when they are not under stress, male narcissists have higher blood levels of stress chemicals. Numerous health problems may arise from this: diabetes, depression, gastrointestinal problems, asthma, and high blood pressure. Furthermore, narcissists are more susceptible to the negative effects of substance addiction in general since they frequently turn to drugs as a means of easing their misery. Lastly, their sense of entitlement will also lead to noncompliance with treatment plans, which can raise their chance of dying, particularly for those with chronic illnesses like cancer that need intensive care. Every person with NPD has an uncertain future because it is a dangerous and difficult mental disorder to treat. In addition, because it is a challenging ailment to diagnose, a person may live their entire life without a diagnosis or treatment. This is especially true if the person suffering from the condition is unaware of their problem. If they do, they could also be difficult to diagnose and cure with medicine. It can be challenging to diagnose NPD because it manifests itself in so many different ways. People who have a specific ailment may also exhibit any of these traits. That is one of the challenges in differentiating between this psychiatric illness's presentations. Moreover, studies indicate that it can be challenging to differentiate between stable and unhealthy narcissism.

Six

They take this action to make sure you don't surpass them. They think everything you do should be done with their happiness in mind. Moreover, they want no one else to have any influence on your life save themselves. They are pathologically jealous because they value their control over you more than anything else. Moreover, when you enjoy wealth and pleasure unconnected to them, they become jealous because they can't follow that inner bliss. Finally, what keeps you from leaving if you can find acceptance elsewhere?

Finding a narcissist is just the beginning. After all, merely realizing someone is a narcissist is insufficient to alter the circumstance. Knowing how a narcissist thinks and feels can help you anticipate their reactions to events, which can help you and others around you prepare for them and effectively resolve, if not completely avoid, confrontations.

Gaining insight into the thoughts of a narcissist will improve your rapport with them. Narcissists are typically associated with love relationships. Nonetheless, the family setting may be the source of the most widespread harm. Scientific research has shown that children raised in narcissistic homes find it difficult to identify problems in their lives. In these kinds of familial interactions, denial is typical.

Originate from the specified group.

Envious of the achievements of others

Example: Marsha can be spiteful, even though it's common to feel jealous of other people's accomplishments, especially when young. A student begins backstabbing her when she is appointed editor-in-chief of the middle school newspaper. Marsha claims that the other girl was named editor-in-chief rather than her because of favoritism.

- Lacks compassion for other kids

For instance, Aaron witnesses a different youngster fall to the ground. The youngster lets forth a cry. Aaron argues that the other youngster is either acting out or is not truly hurt, rather than assisting them. He does not attempt to assist; he just turns and leaves. He listens to other kids when they confide in him about their issues. He is proud of his ability to handle things better than the other kids and feels he has more significant issues than them.

- Quick to take offense at criticism or correction

Example: Leon isn't accustomed to receiving criticism. His mom merely permits him to stay at home. He, therefore, reacts strongly when his teacher corrects him in class. He believes he is correct. It must have taken a keen eye to see that he wasn't cheating. He was just in class asking a friend a question. Leon is going to tell his mother about the teacher's unfairness.

- Not acknowledging mistakes and assigning blame to others

For instance, Flora took a few cookies out of the jar. Since her cousin was going to celebrate a birthday, her mom was furious that she had cooked the cookies for him. She informs her mother that her brother stole the cookies rather than offering an apology. She also intends to get away with it by telling her mother that her brother instructed her to do so they could share.

Narcissistic tendencies can already exist in children. You may have noticed certain names that came to mind when reading about the indicators that someone is more likely to experience NPD in later life.

What concrete or particular factors lead to narcissism?

Divorce/Shattered Houses

People with narcissistic tendencies often think they are in charge. A defenseless child in a dysfunctional household might feel compelled to wear this character as a cloak of protection. Children from shattered households often make it out alive. On the other hand, people who are weak at heart or who have narcissistic tendencies will give in and even fabricate an entirely new backstory. These kids would argue that their parents are still together. Dad travels to numerous countries for work, so he lives somewhere else.

Childhood Unsupervised

A well-supervised but neglected child will also develop his own identity. This person possesses greater maturity and knowledge. They must learn to fend for themselves and put on a stronger defense. Not all people who experience neglect go on to become narcissists. On the other hand, narcissism might surface to defend oneself.

Overindulged Childhood

Youngsters who grow up feeling like they are the center of the universe might not have the opportunity to come down off their high horse. They might even flourish in these dreams as adults, particularly in difficult times. These are kids that never truly grew up. Additionally, they are the narcissists who are most likely to desire to continue living in codependency with others who are close to them.

Maltreatment

Abuse of any kind, including neglect, physical, verbal, emotional, and sexual abuse, can trigger the mind's protection systems. He may opt to use pretending to be the person who has an excessive amount of self-confidence as a protective technique. It's a type of detachment.

Family with Narcissism

Narcissistic parents tend to do #3 to their kids. And there's leading by example. A youngster learns and acts on what they observe.

Molecular Biology

In the most inexplicable cases, heredity might be involved. Oversensitivity is one of the hereditary issues that can arise. Certain families exist that may consistently take things personally. Children learn how to deal with life in those families. Their past experiences can occasionally influence a narcissist's perception of other people.

The remembrance of the handsome man who rejected her love would cause the mountain nymph immense sorrow and embarrassment for the remainder of her life. All left of her would be a faint, hardly discernible echo after she passed away. This was her heartbreak, her soul's echo, experiencing a time of absolute agony.

The goddess of retribution, Nemesis, learns of the tale of Echo, a mountain nymph. Nemesis determines that there is just one thing left to do after sensing the woman's rage and grief. Narcissus is to be punished by Nemesis. One day, Narcissus is thirsty and descends the mountain to obtain water after a demanding and tiring day of hunting high in the woods. Narcissus discovers a water pool. He is unaware that Nemesis had enticed him to this pool rather than him just happening upon it. Bending over, he holds his hands out to catch the first droplets of water that come in contact with his lips. But he comes to an end. He glances into the water, and his eyes enlarge. His desire for anything to drink subsided. Vanished. Rather, such beauty was reflected there in the ocean. The youthful innocence greatly moved Narcissus, and dapper austerity of the young man reflected in the water. Narcissus became fixated on the young man's reflection and realized that the man was, in fact, himself. He could not leave the pool, where he saw his reflection. He was enthralled and realized that no one else could receive the love he held within. Narcissus was so enamored of himself at that moment that he wanted to stare at himself alone. He remained; Nemesis's sentence was served. He lost all sense of existence, and in the exact place where he would finally dry out and perish, a white and golden bloom took the place of his human form.

Gazing at his lovely and youthful reflection at the pool.

The Causes of Narcissism and What Characterizes a Narcissist

There are several ways to examine the roots that entangle people and mold them into selfish individuals. They have underlying problems and have experienced trauma from their early years. It's possible that they were subjected to physical, psychological, or sexual abuse. They may have "grown up" quickly and alone since a parent raised them without responsibility. They might have grown up with a narcissistic parent or sibling, or they might have witnessed a horrifying crime or tragic accident. As a result, they may have absorbed the personality and behaviors of those around them during that formative stage of development, which functions as a sponge. The unlucky and frequently devastating exposure to mature difficulties that leave lasting mental scars is the underlying cause that seeps into a person and fosters the growth of narcissistic behavior. Another possibility is that they were inundated with unmerited praise from the beginning, which gave them the impression that they were perfect and, therefore, had no room for error. This is considered the greatest shortcoming of a narcissist.

Narcissism in youngsters might arise due in part to a parental figure's lack of empathy. Research has indicated that youngsters who experience insufficient affection do not acquire the necessary skills to reciprocate the affection. Since the youngster isn't getting enough attention at home, it is reasonable that this behavior could first appear as a craving for more attention. After that, it may intensify into acting out or flaunting oneself to attract attention. Furthermore, a child may learn that being kind always results in something wonderful. This detracts from being sincere and could lead to a false standard of kindness that is taken for granted.

Draw Attention to Selfishness

You may find it tempting to protect your child from any hazardous situations you encounter while raising them. It might just be your innate desire to shield your kids from harm. Sadly, there is no practical or efficient way to prevent narcissism with this technique. Let the youngster observe the behavior instead. Describe why it is incorrect and what should be done instead. This is a critical component of maturing and acquiring the abilities required for maturity.

7. Narcissistic psychopath

Cerebral or cognitive narcissists cherish their thoughts more than their bodies, in contrast to somatic narcissists, who value their physical appearance.

Cerebral narcissists get their dose from believing they are more intelligent, shrewder, and smarter than other people. Narcissists with a high IQ believe they are far smarter than others. To boost their egos, they will try to make people feel foolish. If you're close to someone who is a cerebral narcissist, shield yourself from their comments.

8. A conceited spiritual

Spiritual narcissists frequently use religious language to intimidate people and use it as an excuse for bad deeds. Young people and those who have recently experienced a significant life transition, like moving or filing for bankruptcy, are particularly vulnerable to the "fascinating, powerful impact" of spiritual narcissists. Remain far from anyone you know who tries to diminish or control you because of their faith.

Several different unique forms of narcissism fall on a spectrum; some of these are more alarming than others. The best ways to protect oneself are to set limits and boundaries and, if possible, leave the connection altogether.

10. Disregarding constraints

One of the most prevalent complaints from victims of narcissistic abuse is the inability to make intelligent decisions, particularly ones that call for a clear distance. The attachment style and physical proximity are two control tactics discussed above. Narcissists enjoy turning the tables on others; thus, they may break the law to stay one step ahead of the game. Further basic norms like being allowed to use the bathroom alone or having the freedom to choose what to dress or eat for one's body are frequently broken. Abusers are accused of reading the notebooks, diaries, or personal emails of their victims.

11. Instilling fear of negative consequences

Narcissistic abusers take great pleasure in displaying signals of fear or anxiety in their victims, knowing that they might be taken advantage of. Victims may display physical fear of the abuser in addition to psychological concern about how to predict or affect the abuser's actions. The victim of abuse may see this as uncertainty because they are paralyzed by fear of making the wrong move or of going beyond the boundaries set by the narcissist. Alternatively, it could turn the victim into their spouse's gofer, who is always trying to meet the demands of the abuser to prevent an outbreak. When the victim does tiresome and humiliating tasks in an attempt to mitigate or fully block their partner's negative feelings, the abuse may become even more evident.

12. Lining up Successful People

Experts claim that regret or embarrassment about past experiences can contribute to narcissism in certain cases. Even as adults, those underlying feelings of insecurity will persist. Because of this, a lot of adult abusers intentionally overaccommodate their victims or attempt to win them over to gain that validation. In an attempt to appear impressive to everyone around them, abusers may apply for jobs or situations regardless of how challenging or unfavorable they are.

13. Excuses for unruly behavior

In addition to not taking counsel effectively, narcissists frequently educate their victims to defend themselves. This suggests that a victim might try to leave even before the narcissist receives criticism. They will either offer an explanation to mitigate the impact, or they will make a minor adjustment and allow the abuser to take full credit.

Someone who has endured long-term abuse may express sentiments such as "Please, don't act on their behalf." You don't know them, as I do. Although they often don't act that way, they are dealing with a lot."

They are often lies. Although victims may be stating this because they genuinely think their partner is excellent, it's usually a self-defense mechanism. To maintain their dignity, narcissists may appear to be able to take criticism well in public, but in private, they may take out their frustrations and anxieties on their victims.

The Influence of Words: Modifying the Internal Narrative

Have you ever given the power of a single word any thought? Think of a term that has previously had an impact on you. It might have been an encouraging comment that made your day, or it might have been a terrible word that broke your heart. Words make up our existence and can construct walls, bridges, and realities. In addition to being how we express our innermost feelings, ideas, and desires, words also help us, whether consciously or unconsciously, to create images of ourselves and the world that we see around us.

What if I told you that you could alter your perspective and the path of your life just by altering the language you speak to yourself and other people? No, I'm not referring to magic here. I am referring to the potent instrument known as neuro-linguistic programming. In "1984" (1949), George Orwell showed us how language control may affect how we perceive the world. You can manage your ideas if you can control your words. However, what if we apply that idea to our benefit?

Self-discovery begins with an awareness of our own language and how it impacts our mental health. NLP allows us to recognize, question, and alter the linguistic patterns that constrain us.

One might wonder why this act of language introspection is so important. Consider it. Our internal reality and, by extension, the narratives shape our exterior reality we tell ourselves and the language we employ to express our experiences. We are the architects of our reality. What happens if we don't like the reality we've made? This is where the internal script has to be modified.

Do you find yourself telling yourself things like "I can't," "I'm not good enough," or "I don't deserve" all the time? Just for a moment, consider the strength, power, and confidence that would result from substituting such phrases with "I can," "I am valuable," and "I deserve the best."

To get you started, consider your all-time favorite film—the one that has enthralled and touched you. The dialogue between the characters and the words in the screenplay define the plot. Similarly, your life narrative is shaped by the words you choose to use.

Before we go any further into this fascinating world of linguistic reconfiguration, let me ask you a very important question: Are you ready to take charge of your story and rewrite your internal script? If the response is affirmative, I can assure you that this experience will equip you with the methods and resources required to change who you are and reclaim your emotional independence. Time to change the storyline. It's time to make a life alteration.

You are about to set off on a voyage rooted in both modern science and history. It is crucial to remember that, as we clear the way, we expose and utilize knowledge that has long been overlooked rather than delving into a novel idea.

In "Syntactic Structures" (1957), Noah Chomsky presented that language is more than just a collection of words and grammatical rules. Instead, it profoundly depicts our thoughts and perceptions of reality. Stated differently, language structures are reflections of our mental systems.

Those who are narcissistic are adept at taking others by surprise. Recall the beginning of your partnership. Did things seem a bit too wonderful to be true at times? Did you consider yourself fortunate to have met someone who coincidentally had all of your interests and aspirations for the future?

Narcissists use mirroring to draw in possible mates. They focus on what you want to hear right away. They then mimic it back to you while making elaborate, amorous motions. This mixture is so addictive that it will quickly get you hooked.

You may later find that the narcissist doesn't share your long-term objectives and isn't interested in your interests.

Unfortunately, you might have established strong sentiments by now that make ending the relationship difficult. Your affection for them can be fully exploited by the narcissist, who will use you as a supply of narcissistic energy until they grow tired of you and move on.

6. They seem indifferent to your feelings, even if they listen to your problems.

A narcissist will make a good show of listening to you if doing so helps them. For instance, if they are just starting in a relationship and want you to think well of them, they might listen while you tell them about your awful workday. However, a narcissist is unable to exhibit any genuine empathy.

They can appear to be simply going through the motions, nodding now and then while they gaze off into the distance. When the narcissist has eventually "won" you over, they'll probably stop acting like they're listening and just shut you out.

7. You find yourself rationalizing away their inappropriate actions.

Seeing your loved one through rose-colored glasses is a common occurrence. It's not always a negative thing. Living with another human being is easier when there is positive bias. But when your desperation to keep the relationship going overrides your ability to see warning signs and harmful habits, it's time to back off.

8. You begin to notice discrepancies in their accounts or discover proof that they lied to you.

Narcissists typically have a poor understanding of reality due to their skewed perception of the world and sick self-image. They might also embellish their account of what happened to impress you or give you a false sense of security. To win your sympathy, they might present you with an altered version of the facts, leading you to believe they were wronged.

To make you feel bad for them, they can, for instance, tell you that their former partner was "abusive" or "crazy." But eventually, you might find out from other sources that the narcissist's abuse was truly directed at their ex.

Because it offers them a sense of power, narcissists could even enjoy tricking you for fun. For example, your significant other may pretend to be at the gym following work, but, in reality, they were out enjoying drinks with a coworker. They might then comment on the bar they visited a few days later.

Narcissistic Abuse Types

• Maltreatment in the Body

When most people think of abuse, they think of this. Physical abuse refers to the application of physical punishment, regardless of whether you are left with a mark. It is considered physical abuse and should not be accepted if the other person ever touches you or puts their hand on you in any way without your permission. In the end, you have the right to control your body, and you have the freedom to choose not to be touched.

- Verbal Mistreatment

You are verbally abused whenever the voice is used in a way that is intended to cause you pain or discredit you. This includes insulting, derogatory, or shouting words directed towards you to cause you pain. A narcissist uses his voice to put you down, but some people may say critical things and utilize them legitimately to help you become a better person. Often, verbal abuse is tolerated because it does not physically harm you, but frequent insults and name-calling can wear you down and negatively impact your mental health for a long time.

Any verbal harm you regard to be deliberate and damaging, such as yelling, demanding, guilt trips, sarcasm, threatening, calling names, insulting, or anything else involving the voice, is considered verbal abuse.

• Abuse of Sexual Relations

Sexual abuse is one of the sneakiest, most harmful kinds of abuse that someone may do to another person. It includes coerced sexual acts or unwanted sexual touching. Sexual abuse can occur even in situations where there is no explicit sexual activity; for example, tapping your butt against your will or making uncomfortable physical contact could qualify.

It's important to keep in mind that being married or in a relationship with someone does not permit them to utilize your body in ways that you find uncomfortable. If it's not consensual, a spouse may sexually abuse the other person. Recall that neither a sleeping person nor a person under the influence of drugs or alcohol can consent to sexual contact. Sexual assault also includes coercing or harassing you into having sex that you do not desire.

- Abuse of Money

You are in some way barred from money when you are the victim of financial abuse. This occurs frequently in abusive couples, usually with one earning all the money and the other staying at home, though this isn't always the case. Regardless of who earns the money, one person seizes control and limits access. The whole idea is to keep the dependant trapped, depending on the abuser to take care of all of their requirements.

This is often accomplished by restricting access through various bank accounts, giving the victim little or nothing to fund basic expenses while keeping the remainder hidden. The abuser may have moved all of your money into an account you cannot access, taken your money and limited your access to it, or used theft to gain control over your resources. Obtaining credit cards in your name and using them to rack up debt and keep you imprisoned is another way to do it. You might be the victim of financial abuse if you do not agree to that arrangement and do not have equal access to the money in your marriage. Some couples decide to divide their finances, but that has to be decided upon jointly.

This indicates that they want to identify that certain quality in others they believe to be a part of themselves. For example, people are drawn to someone who embodies the success, style of dress, and communication style they consider to be their strong points. As a result, they may idealize and fantasize about this person or develop certain expectations of them.

When these demands are not fulfilled, they have a devastating reaction. In their view, the person loses all value and occasionally turns aggressive. In his perspective, narcissists typically have envy for other people. In his perspective, they deserve everything and even more than others. Because narcissists harbor a great deal of envy, it is easy for them to act cunningly and dishonestly in relationships. A narcissist is full of hate and is prone to feel jealous of others. When they cannot command, control, or dominate, they get envious, which grows into hatred. Their lies are the cornerstone of their envy-based foundation, which typically serves as the basis for all their interactions.

The number of professionally qualified individuals being trained to assist those impacted by narcissistic parents is increasing along with awareness of narcissistic personality disorder. This increase, nevertheless, falls well short of the understanding, instruction, and support that the thousands of people suffering from the harsh consequences of narcissistic parents so desperately need. Margolis Felstead, Ph.D., LMFT, is one of those individuals making a name for herself in the field of NPD therapy. She graduated from Oregon State University with a doctorate in Marriage and Family Therapy/Counselling and focuses on helping clients who have narcissistic parents or spouses. In one of her pieces, Margolis lists the following indications as being shared by all narcissists.

Since there are no physical medical procedures that can be used to diagnose narcissism, such as blood tests, MRIs, or X-rays, it is difficult to identify a narcissist. To ascertain whether or not a person is a narcissist, a therapist must examine behavioral patterns.

Psychologists have been asked a lot of questions concerning the inner workings of narcissistic minds and what drives them. Since an individual's thoughts are private and hidden from others, psychologists have spent the last ten years discussing how to ascertain what goes on in the mind of a person, particularly one who has NPD. People with NPD have learned to conceal some repetitive actions and find new ways to show their inner need for care and excessive adoration, even if some behaviors are consistently seen as a regular pattern of how a human mind functions.

It's possible that you were raised by narcissistic parents or relatives your entire life and never gave it any thought that they might be suffering from a psychiatric condition that you could be able to treat if you knew what it was and that it would improve your connection with them. Instead, because you disagreed with your parents' parenting style, you have always had a tense connection with them and have fought and struggled with them. It's not always the case that parents who are rigid or harsh in their parenting are narcissists. All they are trying to do is prevent a child from going down the wrong path.

inclinations

Though it may seem basic, are you aware of your partner's preferences in specific circumstances? Where would they want to go on vacation if they could go anywhere they wanted? Do they enjoy or hate surprises? What is their true opinion on practical jokes? Even though these seem ridiculous, they are very important questions. What would happen if you were to arrange a lavish surprise birthday celebration for your significant other, only to discover that they actually detest surprises and would much rather have a small, private celebration? This can make you feel underappreciated for your work and leave your partner feeling let down. It's true that the idea or thought matters in some cases, but if you've been dating for a while, you ought to be able to come up with something they'd approve of. Maintaining a long-term, fulfilling, and healthy relationship depends critically on understanding your partner's preferences (Getting to know your partner well, n.d.). But the tough thing about preferences is that they shift as we age and experience different things in life. For example, you might have liked going out with friends on Friday nights when you were in your twenties, but now that you're in your thirties, you prefer to watch Netflix and go to bed by ten on Fridays.

The secret to preferences is this:

1. Know before you go: Be sure you know some of your possible partner's fundamental preferences before entering into a relationship. That doesn't mean running a background check or stalking them and their ex-partners on social media; instead, make sure you have enough information to determine whether you want to learn more. Occasionally, we meet someone and get to know them well enough to decide we'd sooner return home. Make sure you

are sufficiently familiar with someone to want them in your life.

2. Know as you go: It's critical to always learn more about your mate since as we mature, our preferences also change. Take some time to reacquaint yourself with each other's tastes and peculiarities, even if you think you already know everything about each other and are contemplating marriage. Adapting and growing is not only healthy, but it also keeps things interesting!

Are you prepared for the questions you will be asked next? Now, let's move!

The Five Abuse Stages

There are five distinct stages to the abuse cycle, each identified by a distinct form of abusive behavior, some of which may not be immediately apparent as abusive. Gaining trust is the initial step, during which the abuser presents the victim as ideal and exhibits nice, caring behavior. This is the time when narcissist presents only the idealized or false version of themselves in cases of narcissistic abuse.

Over-involvement is the second stage, during which the abuser attempts to get to know every aspect of the victim's life.

In the third stage, known as "rulemaking," the abuser uses jealous and domineering behavior to establish the parameters of the partnership. The abuser presents this as a sign of their love for the victim, but it goes well beyond typical relationship uneasiness due to the level of jealousy and micromanaging.

The abuser uses various forms of abuse and manipulation to obtain control over the victim throughout the fourth stage of abuse. At this point, the victim's capacity to notice and react to what is happening has already weakened, and this is when the majority of blatantly abusive acts take place.

In the fifth stage, known as trauma bonding, the abuser temporarily recreates the perfect version of themselves in an attempt to get closer to the victim.

Techniques for Management

Specific abusive actions should be easy to identify if you realize that the manipulative and controlling behaviors of the abuser are part of a pattern. A few of the narcissistic abuser's techniques of control are:

superficially endearing

Bombing someone with love

nagging and ignoring

Penalties

Feeling Remorseful

Blackmailing someone emotionally

Separation

Mental Tricks

Gaslighting

It's the Victim's Fault Superficial Charm

The narcissist's interpretation of courtship conduct is "superficial charm." The charming behavior is a manifestation of the false self the narcissist has built; thus, despite the narcissist's slick and likable exterior, there is nothing real about them. Narcissistic parents may resort to fake charm when interacting with people outside the home, such as teachers or social workers. The narcissist employs flimsy charm in a romantic setting to win the victim over.

Early in a relationship, narcissists can come across as exceptionally romantic, caring, and complimenting. They might give the impression that they know you too well or idealize you. "Ingratiation" is a psychological control strategy when the abuser intentionally mimics your preferences to win your trust.

All of these actions are a part of the act. It might be challenging to distinguish between sincere kindness and surface-level charm, but if your gut tells you something is wrong, you should pause and watch for additional warning signs, such as "love bombing."

Developing a parenting plan or checklist to evaluate the suitability of parents is covered in Chapter 3.

After a separation or divorce, a parenting plan or checklist outlines how parents who do not live together will raise their kids. It also describes how important choices about their kids will be made in both houses. Any parenting arrangement can be agreed upon, but you should prioritize your children's needs. Before you begin, there are a few things you should know.

You might be familiar with legal terms like "custody," "contact," "parenting time," "decision-making responsibility," and "access" to refer to various aspects of child-rearing arrangements, but you don't have to use legal jargon to write your parenting plan; instead, the language you choose should make it clear what you and the other parent have agreed upon. A documented parenting plan is crucial as it documents your decisions jointly regarding the future and can prevent future arguments.

Before signing a parenting plan, consult a family law attorney or lawyer to ensure you know your legal rights and obligations. The agreement is binding in several provinces and territories if both parents sign it. Calling a witness or taking other steps could be necessary in other provinces.

Suppose your parenting plan is included in your Divorce Act order. It needs to be incorporated into the relevant contact order or parenting order. If you're not utilizing the Divorce Act to establish parenting arrangements, you might decide to have your parenting plan put into action.

You may ask that your parenting plan be included in an order subject to provincial or territorial legislation.

This checklist outlines important considerations that you should have when creating your parenting plan. It will help you brainstorm conversation starters with the other parent, like how you will decide on decisions for your children (e.g., jointly or individually) when you spend time with them and how you will communicate and engage with each other.

A parenting plan should take your kids' interests and needs into consideration. It is important to consider the ages of your children and how the plan may change as they grow older. Your plan should have enough complexity to define expectations clearly but be reasonably changeable. Consider how well you can work with the other parent when determining how specific your parenting plan has to be.

The people you know the most about are your children. Keep in mind that some of the items on the checklist might not apply to your situation. Some may remain pertinent to your situation even if they're not on the list.

Many people are unaware of the dangers associated with having a self-centered partner. It's everything but a pleasant relationship because egotists cause their victims a great deal of enthusiastic extortion and suffering. They are also damaging, self-serving, and manipulative.

Narcissistic personality disorder has negative consequences on self-centered people since they require empathy and a real understanding of emotions. Similarly, dealing with arrogant partners can be very confusing since they may be kind to you one day and contemptuous of you the next. Usually, they struggle to decide if they should love you or hate you. As a result, many people who work with egomaniacs witness it and attempt to understand their constant display of heat and cold affection.

Here, we'll examine the egotist's behavior during devotion in greater detail from top to bottom. This can help you determine whether your partner is an egotist and whether you genuinely want to end this toxic relationship.

The Narcissist Love Circle

It's typically past the stage where you recognize you're dealing with an egomaniac. In light of this, being completely separated becomes problematic. Some would have been with the egomaniac for a long time and ought to marry and have children. In addition, some people connect with the toxic connection and develop dependency despite any potential harm from being in a relationship with a narcissist.

Some people may come to believe they are unworthy of greater things and aren't good enough due to the numerous schemes of an egotist. These people have experienced constant mistreatment and have been made to feel worthless, which eventually leads them to adopt this belief.

How Is Loved by a Narcissist?

In contrast to ordinary people, egomaniacs behave differently during moments of affection. We shall examine their loving example below to highlight it. Launching a bait

An egomaniac is usually the best impostor when you go over them from the start. Egotists, with kindness and sincerity, initiate most associations. They'll show you affection and praise. They will make every effort to ensure that you fall at their feet and will arrive with great kindness.

When you first started dating an egomaniac, you might have been utterly certain that you were finally in a relationship with the right person. You don't want it to end because it appears too good to consider embracing. It's possible that you were inundated with compliments, presents, approval, excursions, and dinners that convinced you that you were with your true love and life mate.

Also, Narcissists Are Imprisoned in Their Conundrum

It may sound absurd, but the facts are as follows. You keep replaying this love-hate relationship in your thoughts.

The same actions are taken by narcissists as well. That is the great truth, even though it is difficult to accept. Even if they may act or detest you, they still miss you and want you back.

Have you ever noticed how someone with a predisposition toward narcissism always seems to find a way back to you? They can even randomly show up one day and knock on your door for no apparent reason. They might also send you texts and emails. When you least expect it, they act in that way.

Even after you split up with your narcissistic husband, started a family of your own, and moved away from your narcissistic mother, they will still make small attempts to contact you. It will make you crazy.

Dr. Craig Malkin, author of Rethinking Narcissism, claims that individuals with narcissistic personality disorder (NPD) are in a state of self-trap. Narcissists, according to him, are engaged in a "continuous battle between wanting you and pushing you away."

The way that you display such inner turmoil sets you apart from the narcissist with whom you were in a relationship. For the majority of us who have experienced it, we frequently experience a panic attack and cry for a while.

It will be expressed or manifested in the most bizarre way possible by a narcissist. For example, you will receive an email from them. You will initially believe that they wish to get back in touch. They could even include some nice words in the email. When you read the poem in its entirety, though, you will also encounter derogatory comments.

Recall that communication is two-way in a relationship. You end the connection when it isn't the same. That may also be what the narcissist wants. But you want there to be a significant finality to your departure. On the other hand, the narcissist will not give up easily. You both want the same thing—you just don't agree on how you want the relationship to end.

www.ingramcontent.com/pod-product-compliance
Lightning Source LLC
Chambersburg PA
CBHW052140110526
44591CB00012B/1797